NAVIGATING THE WORLD OF INSTRUCTIONAL DESIGN

Copyright © 2023 by Courtnee R. Morris
Published by Mack N' Morris Entertainment LLC
macknmorris.com

All rights reserved. No part of this book may be reproduced in any manner whatsoever without written permission except in the case of brief quotations embodied in critical articles and reviews.

ISBN: 9781950490714
Ebook ISBN: 9781950490721
First Printing, 2023

Navigating the World of Instructional Design

COURTNEE R. MORRIS

Mack N' Morris Entertainment

Contents

1	Introduction to Instructional Design	6
2	The Foundations of Instructional Design	10
3	Understanding Instructional Design Models	19
4	Analyzing Learning Needs	24
5	Setting Clear Learning Objectives	30
6	Designing Engaging Learning Activities	38
7	Assessing Learning and Progress	44
8	Ensuring Inclusivity in Instructional Design	50
9	The Art and Science of Effective Assessment	55
10	The Evolving Landscape of Educational Technology	61
11	The Power of Gamification in Education	65
12	The Digital Learning Landscape	70
13	The Power of Inclusivity in Education	76
14	Building Collaborative Partnerships in Education	82
15	Evaluating Instructional Design Projects	88
16	Continuous Improvement in Instructional Design	94

About The Author 100

Introduction:

Welcome to the world of instructional design, a realm where education meets innovation, and where learning experiences are crafted to inspire, engage, and transform. In the following pages, we will embark on a journey to explore the art and science of instructional design. We will uncover the secrets of creating effective educational interventions, aligning them with the vision and mission of educational institutions, and diving into strategies and partnerships that enhance learning experiences. Together, we will navigate the vast landscape of educational design, where theory meets practice, and where the future of learning is born.

The Power of Education

In an age defined by information, technology, and the relentless pursuit of knowledge, education stands as a beacon of hope, a gateway to opportunity, and a force that transcends borders and boundaries. It empowers individuals to discover their potential, broadens horizons, and builds bridges across diverse cultures and communities. Education has the power to shape lives, foster understanding, and drive societal progress. It's a dynamic, ever-evolving force that propels individuals and nations toward a brighter, more informed future.

But the world of education is far from static. It is no longer enough to rely on traditional methods and time-worn strategies. The demands of modern society, with its rapid technological advancements and changing societal needs, require education to evolve. Enter instructional design, a field dedicated to the art and science of crafting meaningful learning experiences. It's the guiding hand that ensures education remains not just relevant but also transformative.

The Role of Instructional Design

Instructional design is an essential element of the educational ecosystem, a discipline that combines the insights of psychology, the tools of technology, and the art of pedagogy to create effective learning experiences. Its practitioners, instructional designers, are akin to architects of education. They lay the foundation, design the structure, and construct the pathways that learners follow on their educational journeys.

Instructional designers aren't content with the status quo; they continually seek ways to enhance the learning process. They are champions of creativity and innovation, committed to ensuring that educational interventions are engaging, effective, and relevant. The work of instructional designers influences not just the students' experiences but also the success and reputation of educational institutions.

In this book, we will unravel the multifaceted world of instructional design. We'll dive into the key principles, theories, and methodologies that underpin this field. Together, we'll explore how instructional designers create learning experiences, align them with educational missions, and evaluate their effectiveness. By the end of our journey, you will not only understand the core concepts of instructional design but also appreciate the critical role it plays in shaping the future of education.

Navigating Our Journey

Our exploration of instructional design unfolds across chapters, each looking into a different facet of this dynamic field. Whether you're an experienced instructional designer seeking to refine your approach, an educator intrigued by the art of designing learning experiences, or a curious learner eager to understand how knowledge is crafted, this journey is for you.

As we venture into the world of instructional design, consider the following questions:

> What inspires learners to engage with educational content?
>
> How do educators create impactful learning experiences?
>
> What strategies align learning with broader institutional goals?
>
> How can we evaluate the success of educational interventions?

Our journey will answer these questions and more, providing a holistic perspective on the art and science of instructional design. You'll learn how to design effective educational experiences, align them with institutional missions, and evaluate their impact.

A Roadmap for Learning

Each chapter offers an in-depth exploration of key concepts, supported by practical insights, case studies, and expert perspectives. You'll discover a rich tapestry of ideas and tools that will empower you to create educational interventions that inspire, engage, and transform. Along the way, we will examine the best practices that shape effective learning experiences and the challenges faced in a rapidly evolving educational landscape.

The journey we embark upon will equip you with the knowledge and tools to make a meaningful impact in education, whether you're an instructional designer seeking to refine your craft, an educator aiming to inspire your students, or a lifelong learner eager to understand how knowledge is created and shared.

So, fasten your seatbelt, embrace your curiosity, and prepare to navigate the dynamic world of instructional design. Our journey begins here, but the path stretches far into the future of education, where the possibilities are as limitless as the human quest for knowledge and understanding.

Reflection Questions:

1. What motivates you to explore the world of instructional design? How do you envision this knowledge impacting your role or your learning journey?
2. Reflect on your most memorable learning experiences. What made them stand out? Were they creatively designed, aligned with specific goals, or meticulously evaluated?

3. What challenges or opportunities do you foresee in the field of education, and how can instructional design address them?

Chapter 1

Introduction to Instructional Design

In the realm of education, the path to progress is guided by thoughtful design. It's a journey that starts with a vision and a deep understanding of the learners we aim to serve. This chapter will mark the beginning of our exploration into instructional design, a multifaceted field that lies at the heart of effective education.

Understanding Instructional Design

Instructional design is more than just a process; it's a systematic approach to creating, developing, and delivering educational experiences. Whether in a traditional classroom, a corporate training setting, or a virtual learning environment, the principles of instructional design are ever-present, ensuring that knowledge is not just disseminated but also comprehended, retained, and applied.

At its core, instructional design is about crafting experiences that facilitate learning. It's an intentional process of determining what to teach, how to teach it, and how to assess whether learning has occurred. Every decision, from the choice of content and instructional methods to the design of assessments, is made with the learner's needs and the desired outcomes in mind.

The Educational Landscape

The world of education is constantly evolving. In today's digital age, learning is not confined to the four walls of a classroom. It takes place online, through interactive modules, in hands-on workshops, and in collaborative group sessions. Educators and instructional designers need to adapt to these changes, embracing technology and innovative teaching methods while staying true to the principles of effective instructional design.

Instructional Design in Practice

To understand the essence of instructional design, let's consider a real-world example. Imagine you are part of a team tasked with improving special education programs in your school district. Your goal is to enhance the learning experiences and outcomes of students with disabilities. Where do you begin, and how do you ensure your efforts make a significant impact?

This is where instructional design steps in to serve as your guiding framework. In the chapters that follow, we will dive deep into the process of instructional design. We will explore how to conduct needs assessments, set clear project objectives, select appropriate instructional resources, design effective strategies, create an Individualized Learning Management System (ILMS), implement assessments, and provide professional development. Each step contributes to the overall design of an instructional intervention that will transform the educational landscape for students with disabilities.

The Role of Reflection

Instructional design is as much about planning and execution as it is about reflection. It's a journey that involves continuous refinement. As we embark on this exploration, remember that reflection is a critical component of the process. Each chapter in this book will challenge you to consider how the principles of instructional design can be applied in various educational contexts. Reflect on your experiences and how you might adapt these principles to your unique educational setting.

Reflective Questions:

1. How does instructional design influence your role as an educator or instructional designer in your current context?

2. What are the key challenges you face when it comes to designing effective learning experiences for your students or audience?

3. What are the most significant changes you've observed in education, and how do you see instructional design adapting to these changes?

This chapter is just the beginning of our journey into the world of instructional design. The subsequent chapters will take a closer look at each element of the instructional design process, providing you with a comprehensive toolkit to create meaningful and impactful educational experiences.

Chapter 2

The Foundations of Instructional Design

As we journey deeper into the world of instructional design, it's essential to lay a solid foundation. In this chapter, we will explore the key principles and theories that underpin instructional design, providing you with the knowledge necessary to craft effective learning experiences. Understanding these foundational concepts will guide your instructional design journey and empower you to make informed decisions about how to best meet the needs of your learners.

The Science of Learning

Before we embark on the journey of instructional design, we must first understand the science of learning. Learning is a complex cognitive process, and the way we design instruction can significantly impact its effectiveness. Let's explore some fundamental principles of learning:

1. The Importance of Prior Knowledge

Prior knowledge, what a learner already knows, plays a critical role in the learning process. When designing instruction, it's essential to activate and build upon learners' prior knowledge. If you can connect new information to what your learners already understand, you're more likely to facilitate meaningful learning experiences.

Consider this: If you're introducing a new mathematical concept, it's beneficial to start with a problem or scenario that learners can relate to based on their existing knowledge. By connecting the new concept to their prior knowledge, you create a bridge for comprehension.

2. Cognitive Load Theory

Cognitive load theory addresses the idea that the human brain has a limited capacity for processing information. When instructional materials overload learners with too much new information or complex content, it can hinder learning. Effective instructional designers aim to present content in a way that minimizes cognitive load.

To apply this principle, you might:

> Break complex concepts into smaller, digestible chunks.
>
> Provide clear, concise explanations.

> Use multimedia and visuals to support text-based information.

3. Active Learning

Active learning is an instructional approach that encourages learners to engage with the content actively. Research shows that students retain more knowledge when they participate in the learning process, as opposed to passively absorbing information. Activities such as discussions, problem-solving, and hands-on projects can enhance engagement and comprehension.

For instance, in a history class, instead of solely lecturing on historical events, you can organize debates where students take on the roles of historical figures and discuss the events as if they were part of that time.

Theories of Learning

Numerous **theories of learning** have been developed by educators and psychologists to provide insights into how people learn. These theories help instructional designers understand the underlying processes of learning and inform their design choices. Here are a few influential learning theories:

1. Behaviorism

Behaviorism is based on the idea that learning is the result of a change in behavior. This theory emphasizes observable behaviors and the use of reinforcement to shape desired behaviors. Behaviorism is often associated with teaching methods that use rewards and punishments to motivate and guide learning.

To apply behaviorism in instructional design, you might use techniques like:

> Positive reinforcement, such as rewards for achieving specific learning goals.
>
> Systematic instruction, where learners master a skill or concept through step-by-step guidance.
>
> Frequent assessments to measure behavior changes.

2. Constructivism

Constructivism suggests that learners actively construct their understanding of the world by building on previous experiences and knowledge. In a constructivist approach, learners are encouraged to engage in problem-solving and critical thinking. This theory emphasizes the role of social interaction and collaboration in the learning process.

> To incorporate constructivism in instructional design, you can:
>
> Create opportunities for group activities and discussions.
>
> Encourage learners to explore and discover knowledge independently.

> Develop activities that require learners to apply their understanding to real-world scenarios.

3. Connectivism

Connectivism is a relatively modern learning theory that acknowledges the impact of technology on how we learn. It asserts that learning occurs through connecting to networks, both human and technological. In the digital age, information is readily accessible, the ability to find and connect to relevant resources is a crucial skill.

To integrate connectivism into instructional design, you might:

> Emphasize digital literacy skills and online research techniques.
>
> Encourage learners to explore online communities and resources for learning.
>
> Design courses that leverage technology to facilitate collaboration and resource sharing.

The Role of Motivation

Motivation is a driving force in learning. It's the energy that fuels our desire to explore, understand, and engage with new information. In the context of instructional design, understanding motivation is essential. Here are some motivation factors to consider:

1. Intrinsic vs. Extrinsic Motivation

Intrinsic motivation comes from within; it's the innate desire to learn for the sake of learning. Extrinsic motivation, on the other hand, is driven by external factors such as rewards or grades. Effective instructional designers strive to cultivate intrinsic motivation whenever possible.

To promote intrinsic motivation, you can:

> Create learning experiences that tap into learners' curiosity.
>
> Provide choices and autonomy in the learning process.
>
> Offer opportunities for learners to see the real-world relevance of what they are learning.

2. Goal Setting

Goal setting is a powerful motivator. When learners set specific, achievable goals, they are more likely to remain focused and persistent in their efforts. Instructional designers can harness the power of goal setting by incorporating clear objectives into their materials and providing opportunities for learners to set their goals.

For instance, in a language learning program, learners might set goals for the number of vocabulary words they want to master each week.

The Importance of Assessment

Assessment is a fundamental component of instructional design. It allows educators to measure and evaluate learning outcomes. Assessments serve various purposes, from gauging the effectiveness of instruction to guiding learners toward improvement. Here, we'll explore the significance of assessment in the instructional design process:

1. Formative Assessment

Formative assessment occurs throughout the learning process. It's designed to provide feedback that informs and guides instruction, helping learners understand where they are in their learning journey and what adjustments are needed.

Examples of formative assessments include:

> Quizzes and polls during a lesson to check for comprehension.
>
> Class discussions to gauge understanding and encourage participation.
>
> Peer and self-assessment activities that promote reflection on one's own learning progress.

The key to formative assessment is that it's not about assigning grades but about enhancing learning. It's a diagnostic tool for both learners and instructors.

2. Summative Assessment

Summative assessment, in contrast, is typically conducted at the end of a learning period to evaluate the learners' overall understanding and achievement. It determines

whether learning objectives have been met and usually results in a grade or a certification.
Examples of summative assessments include:

> End-of-chapter exams.
>
> Final projects or presentations.
>
> Standardized tests to assess a broad set of knowledge or skills.

Summative assessments provide a clear picture of what learners have accomplished and can help validate the effectiveness of the instructional design.

Reflection Questions

As we wrap up this chapter on the foundations of instructional design, take a moment to reflect on the following questions:

1. How does understanding the science of learning, including cognitive processes and learning theories, impact your approach to instructional design?

2. What are some strategies to promote intrinsic motivation and goal setting within your instructional materials? How can you inspire learners to be more self-driven in their learning?

3. In your current role or future endeavors as an instructional designer, how will you incorporate formative and summative assessments to enhance the

learning experience and evaluate learning outcomes effectively?

These questions serve as food for thought as we progress through this journey of understanding instructional design. In the chapters that follow, we'll look into practical strategies, tools, and best practices that will help you create engaging and effective learning experiences for your students or audience.

Chapter 3

Understanding Instructional Design Models

Instructional design is both an art and a science, and like any field, it relies on a set of principles, models, and frameworks to guide its practice. In this chapter, we explore various instructional design models that provide structured approaches for designing effective learning experiences. We will uncover how these models can serve as valuable blueprints to craft engaging and meaningful educational content.

Introduction to Instructional Design Models

Instructional design models offer a systematic framework for creating educational experiences. They help ensure that the resulting instruction is effective, efficient, and appealing to learners. There are numerous instructional design models, each with its unique characteristics, but all share common fundamental goals:

> **Aligning Objectives:** Models help in clearly defining instructional goals and objectives. This alignment ensures that the instruction is purposeful and contributes to desired learning outcomes.
>
> **Systematic Design:** Models provide a structured approach, ensuring that nothing essential is overlooked in the instructional design process. A systematic approach minimizes errors and enhances the quality of instruction.
>
> **Fostering Learner Engagement:** Effective models place a strong emphasis on engaging learners. Engaged learners are more likely to be motivated and, as a result, achieve better learning outcomes.

In this chapter, we'll dive into some prominent instructional design models, including:

1. ADDIE Model

The **ADDIE model** is perhaps one of the most recognized instructional design models. ADDIE stands for Analysis, Design, Development, Implementation, and Evaluation. Each phase of the model represents a stage in the instructional design process:

Analysis: In this phase, designers identify the learning needs, goals, and objectives. They conduct a thorough analysis of the target audience and existing learning materials.

Design: The design phase involves creating detailed plans for instruction. This includes defining learning objectives, selecting suitable instructional methods, and crafting assessment strategies.

Development: During development, instructional materials are created. This phase can include content creation, curriculum development, and the production of learning resources.

Implementation: Once the materials are developed, the instruction is delivered to learners. Implementation includes the delivery of lessons, workshops, or e-learning modules.

Evaluation: After implementation, designers evaluate the effectiveness of the instruction. They collect feedback, assess whether objectives were met, and make any necessary revisions.

2. Bloom's Taxonomy

Bloom's Taxonomy is a framework that classifies learning objectives into a hierarchy. It consists of six cognitive domains, each representing a different level of cognitive complexity:

Knowledge
Comprehension
Application

> Analysis
> Synthesis
> Evaluation

Educators use Bloom's Taxonomy to ensure that learning objectives align with the desired level of cognitive challenge. For instance, they can use lower-level objectives (e.g., Knowledge or Comprehension) for foundational knowledge and higher-level objectives (e.g., Analysis or Synthesis) for more advanced learning.

3. SAM (Successive Approximation Model)

The **Successive Approximation Model** is a relatively new instructional design model. It focuses on rapid prototyping and cycles of formative evaluation. SAM consists of three phases:

> **Preparation:** This phase sets the groundwork for design, including defining project goals and expectations.
>
> **Iterative Design:** In this phase, designers create prototypes and receive feedback. The cycle of designing, prototyping, and testing repeats until the project reaches the desired quality.
>
> **Implementation:** After the design phase is complete, the project moves to implementation.

Understanding instructional design models is essential for crafting effective learning experiences. Each model brings its unique strengths to the table, making it important for instructional designers to choose the model that best aligns with their goals and learners' needs.

Reflection Questions

1. Have you previously worked with any instructional design models or frameworks? If so, which ones, and how did they impact your instructional design process?

2. How can the ADDIE model benefit your current or future instructional design projects? What elements of the ADDIE model resonate with your instructional design philosophy?

3. Bloom's Taxonomy provides a structured approach to setting learning objectives. How can you leverage this framework to design instruction that encourages higher-order thinking skills in your learners?

Chapter 4

Analyzing Learning Needs

Understanding the learning needs of your audience is a fundamental step in instructional design. Without a comprehensive grasp of what your learners require and how they learn best, creating effective educational experiences becomes a challenging task. In this chapter, take a look at the importance of analyzing learning needs, the methods to do so, and how they shape the design of successful instruction.

The Significance of Learning Needs Analysis

Imagine setting out on a road trip without a map or a GPS. You might eventually reach your destination, but the journey will be filled with detours, delays, and potential frustrations. In the world of instructional design, the learning needs analysis serves as your map, guiding you to create purposeful and effective learning experiences.

Here's why learning needs analysis is pivotal:

Learner-Centric Approach: Analyzing learning needs puts the focus squarely on the learner. By understanding their needs, motivations, and prior knowledge, you can design instruction that speaks directly to them.

Customization: One size doesn't fit all. Different learners have different needs. By conducting a learning needs analysis, you can tailor your instruction to meet these diverse requirements.

Efficiency: Time and resources are precious in the instructional design process. An analysis ensures that you're investing these resources where they're needed most, thereby optimizing the instructional design process.

Now, let's explore the methods and processes of learning needs analysis.

Methods of Learning Needs Analysis

The process of learning needs analysis typically involves various methods and techniques. Here are some commonly employed methods and techniques:

Surveys and Questionnaires: These can be distributed to learners and educators to gather insights into their preferences, gaps in knowledge, and specific needs. Surveys can be especially helpful for identifying overarching trends within a large audience.

Interviews: Conducting one-on-one or group interviews provides an opportunity to dive deeper into the perspectives and experiences of learners. They can offer valuable qualitative insights into learning needs.

Focus Groups: Focus groups bring small groups of learners together for discussions. These conversations can reveal shared concerns, expectations, and desires related to instruction.

Observations: Observing learners in their natural learning environments can provide insights into how they interact with content and resources. Observations are especially valuable for understanding context and learning behaviors.

Performance Data: Analyzing data related to learner performance can help identify areas where learners struggle or excel. Assessments, tests, and course evaluations are examples of performance data sources.

Task Analysis: This method involves breaking down the tasks or skills that learners need to acquire. It helps in identifying what learners must know and do to achieve competence.

Review of Existing Content: Analyzing current learning materials, textbooks, or resources can help you identify gaps and areas that need improvement. It's also an opportunity to build on existing knowledge and experience.

Once you've gathered data through one or more of these methods, the next step is to analyze it thoroughly. This analysis should aim to answer the following questions:

> What are the specific learning objectives and goals?
>
> What do learners need to know or be able to do after completing the instruction?
>
> What are the potential challenges and obstacles learners might face?
>
> What resources are already available, and what needs to be created?
>
> How do learners prefer to learn (e.g., through visual aids, hands-on activities, group discussions, etc.)?

By answering these questions, you can develop a comprehensive picture of your learners and their needs, which will serve as the foundation for designing effective instruction.

Shaping the Design

Once you've conducted a thorough learning needs analysis, you'll have a clear understanding of what your learners require. This information allows you to make informed decisions about the instructional content, methods, and strategies you will employ. The learning needs analysis helps in shaping the design in the following ways:

> Defining Learning Objectives: Based on the learning needs analysis, you can articulate clear and specific learning objectives. These objectives outline what learners should achieve by the end of the instruction.

Selecting Appropriate Content: The analysis informs content selection. It helps you determine what content is necessary and what can be omitted. This ensures that instruction remains relevant and focused.

Choosing Instructional Strategies: You can now decide on the best methods and strategies to deliver content. Whether it's through lectures, hands-on activities, or e-learning modules, your choice is guided by the needs of your learners.

Tailoring Assessments: The analysis allows you to develop assessments and evaluations that align with the learning objectives. It ensures that the assessments accurately measure the knowledge and skills learners need to acquire.

Considering Accessibility: By conducting a learning needs analysis, you can identify accessibility requirements. This could involve creating materials that accommodate learners with disabilities or ensuring content is available in multiple formats.

Creating a Motivating Learning Environment: Understanding learners' motivations and challenges allows you to create an engaging and supportive learning environment. This can include addressing potential barriers and providing appropriate resources and support.

The learning needs analysis is a cornerstone of effective instructional design. It's a step that connects the instructional designer with the learner, making sure that educational experiences are not just efficient but also engaging and purposeful.

Reflection Questions

1. Have you ever participated in a learning needs analysis as either an instructional designer or a learner? What was your experience, and what insights did it provide?

2. Reflect on a learning experience where the instruction seemed disconnected from your needs. How could a learning needs analysis have improved that experience?

3. As an instructional designer, how can you ensure that the learning needs analysis process remains dynamic and adaptable, accommodating the evolving needs of learners and the changing educational landscape?

Chapter 5

Setting Clear Learning Objectives

In the previous chapters, we emphasized the importance of understanding your learners and their needs. Armed with this knowledge, you're now ready to tackle another essential aspect of instructional design: setting clear learning objectives. Learning objectives are the backbone of any instructional program. They serve as guiding beacons, shaping the content, methods, and assessments of your instruction. In this chapter, we'll explore the art and science of crafting precise and effective learning objectives.

The Role of Learning Objectives

Imagine you're embarking on a cross-country road trip. Your first step is deciding on the destination. Similarly, in the world of instructional design, learning objectives represent the destination for your learners. They define where your learners should arrive at the end of the instructional journey.

Learning objectives serve several vital functions:

> **Clarity:** Learning objectives provide clarity. They articulate precisely what learners should know or be able to do by the end of the instruction.
>
> **Focus:** Objectives help in setting clear boundaries for instruction. They ensure that the content remains relevant and doesn't veer off course.
>
> **Assessment:** Learning objectives guide the creation of assessments. They define the criteria by which you can evaluate whether learners have met the objectives.
>
> **Motivation:** Well-crafted objectives can also motivate learners. When learners understand what they are working towards, they are more likely to stay engaged and committed to the instruction.

Types of Learning Objectives

Learning objectives can be classified into different types, each serving a specific purpose in instructional design:

1. Cognitive Objectives

Cognitive objectives relate to intellectual skills and knowledge. They encompass a spectrum of thinking, from basic recall of facts to higher-order thinking like analysis and evaluation. Cognitive objectives might include:

> **Knowledge:** Identifying key terms or facts.
>
> **Comprehension:** Summarizing, interpreting, or explaining information.
>
> **Application:** Applying knowledge to solve problems or complete tasks.
>
> **Analysis:** Breaking down information into its component parts.
>
> **Synthesis:** Combining information in new ways to create something unique.
>
> **Evaluation:** Making judgments or decisions based on criteria.

2. Affective Objectives

Affective objectives center on emotions, attitudes, and values. They are about changing how learners feel or perceive something. Affective objectives might include:

> **Receiving:** Being aware or open to new information.
>
> **Responding:** Showing a reaction or willingness to participate.
>
> **Valuing:** Demonstrating commitment or acceptance of new ideas.
>
> **Organization:** Prioritizing values and resolving conflicts.

> Characterization: Demonstrating consistent behavior and attitudes.

3. Psychomotor Objectives

Psychomotor objectives pertain to physical skills and actions. These objectives focus on what learners can do with their bodies. Psychomotor objectives might include:

> Imitation: Copying a demonstrated skill.
>
> Manipulation: Using dexterity to perform precise actions.
>
> Precision: Refining skills for accuracy and control.
>
> Articulation: Combining skills fluently and effectively.

Writing Effective Learning Objectives

Creating clear and effective learning objectives is a skill that instructional designers must master. Well-crafted objectives serve as the cornerstone of your instructional plan. Let's explore how to write them effectively.

1. Be Specific

Objectives should be specific and unambiguous. They must clearly state what learners are expected to achieve. Vague or general objectives leave room for confusion. Consider the difference between these two objectives:

> Vague Objective: "Understand the principles of physics."
>
> Specific Objective: "Calculate the velocity of an object in freefall based on gravitational acceleration."

A specific objective clearly defines the action that learners must take.

2. Use Action Verbs

Action verbs are critical in learning objectives. They indicate what learners will do to demonstrate their understanding. A well-known framework for using action verbs is Bloom's Taxonomy. This taxonomy categorizes objectives by cognitive level and suggests appropriate verbs for each level. For example:

> Knowledge: Define, identify, list.
>
> Comprehension: Describe, explain, summarize.
>
> Application: Apply, construct, use.
>
> Analysis: Analyze, compare, differentiate.
>
> Synthesis: Create, design, organize.
>
> Evaluation: Assess, critique, justify.

Using the right action verb for your objective ensures that it is specific and measurable.

3. Ensure Measurability

Learning objectives must be measurable. This means they should enable you to determine whether the objective has been met. Consider this objective:

> **Unmeasurable Objective:** "Appreciate the beauty of classical music."
> How would you measure someone's appreciation of classical music? You can't. Now, compare it to this measurable objective:
> **Measurable Objective:** "Identify and explain the elements of classical music in a listening exercise."
> This objective specifies a clear action (identifying and explaining) and the criteria for measurement (elements of classical music).

4. Align with Bloom's Taxonomy

Consider the cognitive level of your objectives. Depending on your instructional context, you might need objectives at different cognitive levels. For example, introductory material may focus on knowledge and comprehension, while advanced courses may aim for application and analysis. Ensure your objectives align with the appropriate cognitive level.

5. Keep Them Attainable

Objectives should be challenging but attainable. Don't set objectives that are so difficult that learners become frustrated, or so easy that they disengage due to lack of challenge.

Now that you understand the structure of effective learning objectives, here's a practical framework to guide you in writing them:

Action Verb + Task + Criteria for Success

> For example:
>
> - "Analyze a case study of patient symptoms to identify the underlying medical condition accurately."
>
> Here, the action verb is "analyze," the task is "a case study of patient symptoms," and the criteria for success is "to identify the underlying medical condition accurately."

Reflection Questions

1. Reflect on your past experiences as a learner. How did having clear learning objectives impact your motivation and understanding of the material?

2. Imagine you're designing a course. Can you identify the different types of learning objectives (cognitive, affective, psychomotor) that might be relevant to different sections of the course? What are some examples of objectives for each type?

3. Share an example of an objective you've encountered in your learning experiences that was not effectively

written. How could it have been improved to make it more specific and measurable?

Chapter 6

Designing Engaging Learning Activities

In the previous chapters, we've journeyed through the essential steps of instructional design, from understanding your learners and setting clear objectives to crafting effective assessments. Now, we arrive at a pivotal point in the process - designing engaging learning activities. These activities are the heart of your instruction, where learners interact with the content and deepen their understanding. In this chapter, we will explore the art of creating activities that captivate learners' attention and foster meaningful learning experiences.

The Significance of Learning Activities

Learning activities breathe life into your instructional content. They transform information from mere facts and figures into active and memorable experiences. Well-designed activities can make the difference between disinterested students and engaged learners who retain and apply what they've learned.

Effective learning activities have several critical functions:

> **Engagement:** Activities capture learners' attention, making the content more engaging and exciting.
>
> **Application:** Activities provide opportunities for learners to apply their knowledge or practice new skills.
>
> **Comprehension:** Hands-on activities can enhance comprehension by making abstract concepts concrete.
>
> **Retention:** Active learning fosters better memory retention, as learners are actively participating in the learning process.
>
> **Problem-Solving:** Many activities are structured to promote problem-solving skills, which are valuable in real-world situations.

Types of Learning Activities

Learning activities come in various forms, depending on the nature of the content and your instructional goals. Here are some common types:

> **Hands-On Activities:** These activities involve physical engagement with the learning material. Examples include experiments, simulations, and interactive labs. For instance, a science class might use hands-on activities to allow students to conduct chemistry experiments.

Group Discussions: Group activities promote collaboration and foster interpersonal skills. Learners discuss a topic or solve problems together. These can include debates, brainstorming sessions, or peer review workshops.

Case Studies: Case studies are detailed examinations of a particular subject or scenario. Learners analyze a situation, identify problems, and propose solutions. These are widely used in fields like business and healthcare.

Problem-Based Learning (PBL): PBL presents learners with a real-world problem to solve. They must apply their knowledge to find a solution. PBL is often used in medical education to prepare students for diagnosing patients.

Role-Playing: Role-playing activities ask learners to assume a particular role or character and engage in a simulated scenario. These activities are common in communication and leadership training.

Interactive Quizzes and Games: Gamified activities use game elements like competition, challenges, and rewards to make learning enjoyable. Digital quizzes and games can be effective tools for reinforcing knowledge.

Creative Projects: Creative projects are open-ended activities that allow learners to express themselves. They can include research papers, art projects, or multimedia presentations.

Designing Engaging Learning Activities

To design effective learning activities, consider these key principles:

Alignment with Objectives

Learning activities should directly align with your learning objectives. Each activity should contribute to achieving one or more objectives. If an activity doesn't support your objectives, it risks becoming a distraction.

Engagement

Engagement is at the core of any effective activity. You want learners to be excited, curious, and motivated to participate. Think about how to spark their interest. Use a variety of media, incorporate storytelling, and make the activity relevant to their lives.

Clear Instructions

Clear and concise instructions are vital. Learners should understand what is expected of them and how to complete the activity. Ambiguity can lead to confusion and frustration.

Varied Formats

Diverse activity formats cater to different learning styles. Some learners excel in hands-on activities, while others prefer reflective exercises. Consider offering a mix of activity types to accommodate various preferences.

Sequencing from Simple to Complex

For a more profound understanding, start with simple activities and gradually introduce more complex ones. This scaffolding approach ensures learners build on their knowledge and skills progressively.

Assessment

> Activities should include mechanisms for assessing learner progress and understanding. Whether through self-assessment, peer review, or instructor evaluation, feedback helps learners gauge their performance.
>
> Flexibility
>
> Flexibility allows learners to explore and adapt the activity based on their interests and needs. While structured activities have their place, offering some room for customization can be empowering.

The Role of Technology

Technology has transformed the landscape of learning activities in education. Digital tools and platforms provide opportunities for interactive and engaging learning experiences. From online simulations and virtual reality to discussion forums and e-learning modules, technology offers a wide array of options to enhance learning activities.

Reflection Questions

1. Think back to a memorable learning experience you've had. What was it about the activities in that learning context that made it engaging and effective?

2. If you were designing a learning activity for a complex topic, how would you ensure that it aligns with the learning objectives and progressively introduces

learners to the content? Can you think of any real-world examples of this approach?

3. As technology continues to shape the educational landscape, how might you incorporate digital tools and platforms into learning activities to enhance engagement and interactivity for learners?

Chapter 7

Assessing Learning and Progress

In our journey through the instructional design process, we've navigated many vital components, from understanding learners to crafting engaging learning activities. Now, we come to a pivotal phase—assessing learning and progress. Assessment is the compass that guides our instructional journey. It helps us understand where our learners are, where they need to be, and how we can bridge that gap effectively.

The Significance of Assessment

Assessment serves a multitude of purposes in education. It provides insights into learners' understanding, informs instructional decision-making, and evaluates the effectiveness of the instruction. Let's look at the significance of assessment:

Measuring Learning: Assessments allow us to measure what learners have gained from the instruction. We can evaluate their knowledge, skills, and abilities related to the learning objectives.

Feedback and Improvement: Assessment provides learners with feedback, highlighting their strengths and areas needing improvement. It serves as a guide for further learning.

Accountability: In many educational settings, assessments are used for accountability purposes, such as grading, certification, or accreditation.

Adaptation: Through formative assessments, instructors can adapt instruction based on learners' needs. If a formative assessment reveals that learners are struggling with a specific concept, the instructor can revisit and clarify that topic.

Validation: Assessments help validate the effectiveness of the instruction. They answer questions like: Did the instruction meet its objectives? Were the learners engaged? Did they gain the intended knowledge or skills?

Motivation: Well-designed assessments can motivate learners to engage with the content and take their learning seriously. The knowledge that they will be assessed often compels them to study and practice.

Types of Assessments

Assessments come in various forms, each serving a specific purpose in gauging learning. Here are some common types of assessments:

Formative Assessment: Formative assessments occur throughout the learning process. They provide feedback to both learners and instructors, helping to identify areas that need improvement. Examples include quizzes, in-class discussions, and peer evaluations.

Summative Assessment: Summative assessments are typically given at the end of an instructional period. They evaluate overall learning outcomes and determine whether learners have met the objectives. Examples include final exams, standardized tests, and end-of-term projects.

Performance Assessment: Performance assessments require learners to demonstrate their skills in real-world contexts. For instance, a medical student might take a practical exam to showcase their clinical skills.

Self-Assessment: Self-assessment encourages learners to reflect on their own understanding and performance. Methods can include self-checklists, journals, or personal goal setting.

Peer Assessment: In peer assessment, learners assess each other's work or performance. This encourages critical thinking and peer collaboration. For instance, students in a writing class might review and provide feedback on each other's essays.

Portfolio Assessment: Portfolio assessments compile a body of work or evidence of learning over time. Learners assemble a collection of their best work, reflecting their progress and achievement. This is common in creative fields like art and design.

Authentic Assessment: Authentic assessments mirror real-life situations. They evaluate learners' abilities to apply their knowledge and skills in practical, meaningful contexts. For instance, an engineering student might be tasked with solving an authentic engineering problem.

Designing Effective Assessments

Designing effective assessments is an art in itself. Assessments should align with your learning objectives, be fair, and provide a clear picture of what learners have learned. Here are some principles to guide your assessment design:

Clarity of Purpose: Assessments should have a clear and specific purpose. What do you want to measure? Make sure your assessment aligns with your learning objectives.

Validity and Reliability: Validity ensures that the assessment measures what it's supposed to. Reliability ensures consistency; the assessment should provide consistent results if repeated. These are fundamental to assessment quality.

Clear Instructions: Learners should understand what is expected of them. Provide clear instructions and rubrics to guide their efforts.

Fairness and Equity: Assessments should be fair to all learners, free from bias, and accessible. Ensure that no learner is disadvantaged due to factors unrelated to the learning objectives.

Variety: Use a variety of assessment types. Different assessments provide different insights into learning. A combination of formative and summative assessments often yields a comprehensive view.

> **Feedback:** Provide meaningful feedback to learners. Feedback should not only reveal their mistakes but also guide them on how to improve.
>
> **Timely Assessment:** Assess learning when it matters most. Timely assessments allow learners to apply feedback and improve while there's still an opportunity.
>
> **Adaptation:** If formative assessments reveal that learners are struggling with a specific topic, be ready to adapt your instruction. This responsiveness is a hallmark of effective teaching.

Technology and Assessment

Technology has significantly impacted the assessment landscape. Digital tools and platforms provide various assessment options, from online quizzes and interactive simulations to automated grading and data analytics. These tools not only streamline assessment processes but also provide rich data for instructors to make data-driven decisions.

Reflection Questions

1. Think about a recent learning experience. What types of assessments were used? How did they contribute to your learning? Did any assessment stand out as particularly effective or ineffective?

2. How do assessments align with learning objectives? Can you think of any examples where assessments and learning objectives seemed mismatched?

3. Consider how technology has influenced assessment. What are the advantages and disadvantages of technology-assisted assessments, and can you identify any areas where technology could enhance assessment in your context?

Chapter 8

Ensuring Inclusivity in Instructional Design

In our journey through instructional design, we've explored numerous facets of creating effective and engaging learning experiences. We've learned about understanding learners, crafting content, designing assessments, and more. However, one core principle underlies all these elements, and it's a principle that we must champion in every aspect of our work—ensuring inclusivity.

The Imperative of Inclusivity

Inclusivity is not just a buzzword. It's a foundational concept that underpins education in its entirety. Inclusive education aims to provide equitable learning opportunities for all, irrespective of differences, disabilities, or other factors. But it's not limited to classrooms alone; it extends to every learning environment we design.

Why Inclusivity Matters

> **Promotes Diversity:** Inclusivity celebrates diversity. It acknowledges that our learners come from different backgrounds, cultures, abilities, and experiences. By embracing this diversity, we enrich the learning experience.
>
> **Ensures Equal Access:** Every learner should have equal access to quality education. Inclusivity removes barriers to learning, ensuring that no one is excluded from the educational process.
>
> **Fosters Empathy:** Inclusive education fosters empathy and understanding. When learners interact with peers from various backgrounds, they gain valuable life skills, including empathy, tolerance, and respect for others.
>
> **Enhances Learning:** Inclusive education can enhance learning for everyone. It encourages cooperative learning and peer support, creating a positive and supportive learning environment.
>
> **Prepares for Life:** Inclusivity mirrors the real world. In life, we encounter people from diverse backgrounds, and inclusive education prepares learners to navigate these real-world scenarios effectively.

Designing Inclusive Learning

Creating inclusive learning experiences involves several aspects:

> **Universal Design for Learning (UDL):** UDL principles guide the creation of instructional materials that can be accessed, understood, and used to the fullest extent by all learners. It recognizes that one size does not fit all and encourages multiple means of representation, engagement, and expression.
>
> **Accessible Content:** Make sure your content is accessible to all. Consider providing alternative text for images, using readable fonts, and ensuring content is navigable using assistive technologies.
>
> **Language and Communication:** Use clear and straightforward language. Avoid jargon or idioms that may be confusing to learners with diverse language backgrounds. For those who are non-native speakers, this can make a significant difference.
>
> **Cultural Sensitivity:** Be mindful of cultural differences. Include a variety of cultural perspectives in your content to avoid a one-sided view of the world.
>
> **Accommodations and Flexibility:** Offer accommodations for learners with specific needs, whether related to disabilities, language proficiency, or other factors. Examples would be written transcripts or captions for video content, extra time for assignments, and translation tools. Also, allow for flexibility in your assignments and assessments, including submission of projects in different formats (videos, slideshows, or papers), choice of questions to demonstrate understanding and distraction-free environments.

> **Inclusive Assessment:** Ensure your assessment methods are inclusive. Consider different ways of assessing learners, and provide opportunities for them to demonstrate their knowledge and skills in various forms.

Challenges to Inclusivity

While inclusivity is a noble goal, it comes with challenges. These include:

> **Limited Awareness:** Sometimes, educators and instructional designers may not fully understand the concept of inclusivity or its importance.
>
> **Resource Constraints:** Limited resources can be a barrier to providing the necessary accommodations and support for learners with diverse needs.
>
> **Resistance to Change:** Change can be met with resistance. Some educators may be resistant to adopting new, more inclusive practices.
>
> **Bias and Stereotypes:** Bias and stereotypes can undermine inclusivity. Educators must be aware of their biases and strive to treat all learners fairly.

Reflection Questions

1. Think about the most inclusive learning experience you've had. What made it inclusive, and how did it impact your learning?

2. In your work or educational setting, what barriers or challenges to inclusivity have you observed? What strategies can help overcome these challenges?

3. Consider an instructional design project you're involved in or planning. How can you ensure inclusivity is embedded throughout the design process, from understanding your learners to creating accessible content and assessments?

Chapter 9

The Art and Science of Effective Assessment

In our journey through the world of instructional design, we've dove into the intricacies of understanding learners, crafting engaging content, and fostering inclusivity in learning experiences. Yet, we've left a critical piece of the puzzle to explore—the art and science of effective assessment.

The Role of Assessment

Assessment is the heartbeat of learning. It's the compass that guides both educators and learners. Effective assessments help educators gauge how well learners are mastering the content and whether the instructional strategies are on target. For learners, assessments provide valuable feedback, helping them understand their progress and areas for improvement.

Assessment's Dual Purpose

> **Summative Assessment:** These assessments come at the end of a learning period to evaluate overall comprehension. They're like the final stroke on a canvas, representing the complete picture. Examples include final exams, end-of-course projects, and standardized tests.
>
> **Formative Assessment:** These assessments occur throughout the learning journey, allowing learners and educators to adjust and adapt in real-time. They're like brushstrokes forming the artwork, shaping its development. Examples include quizzes, peer assessments, and discussions.

Art and Science

The effectiveness of assessments is both art and science. It's the art of designing questions and tasks that elicit meaningful responses. It's the science of using reliable and valid methods to ensure assessment results reflect true understanding.

The Art of Crafting Questions

Clarity: The clarity of questions is paramount. Ambiguity leads to confusion and misinterpretation. Clear questions enable learners to express their knowledge accurately.

Diversity: Like an artist's palette, questions should vary in type. Use a mix of multiple-choice, short answer, essays, and practical tasks to capture different dimensions of learning.

Relevance: Questions should align with learning objectives. They need to be connected to what learners are expected to know and be able to do.

Challenge: Thought-provoking questions challenge learners to think critically and apply their knowledge. The right amount of challenge keeps learners engaged and promotes deep learning.

The Science of Assessment

Reliability: Reliable assessments produce consistent results. If the same learner takes the same test multiple times, the scores should be consistent. Reliable assessments are like scales that provide consistent readings.

Validity: Valid assessments measure what they are supposed to measure. An effective assessment of mathematics knowledge should not unintentionally measure language proficiency.

Fairness: Assessments should be fair to all learners, regardless of their background, culture, or ability. The science of fairness ensures that learners' scores should not influenced by external factors.

Feedback: Effective assessments provide timely and constructive feedback. This feedback is essential for learners to understand their strengths and areas for growth.

Assessing Diverse Learners

In our diverse world, learners come with a wide range of abilities, backgrounds, and preferences. Effective assessments consider this diversity and strive to be equitable.

Universal Design for Assessment (UDA)

Clarity in Language: Use straightforward language. Avoid idiomatic expressions or complex sentence structures that could confuse learners who are non-native speakers.

Flexible Response Formats: Allow for a variety of response formats. Some learners may struggle with written essays but excel in visual projects or oral presentations.

Multiple Assessment Methods: Use a mix of assessment methods to cater to diverse talents and abilities. Ensure that assessment methods are accessible to all.

The Challenges of Assessment

As with every aspect of instructional design, assessment comes with its challenges. These include:

> **Cheating and Plagiarism:** Addressing academic dishonesty in assessments requires vigilance and creative solutions.
>
> **Standardization vs. Personalization:** Balancing standardized assessments with personalized learning is an ongoing challenge. One-size-fits-all assessments may not capture the individual progress of learners.
>
> **Assessment Anxiety:** Some learners experience anxiety during assessments. Identifying and addressing this issue is crucial for equitable learning.
>
> **Data Overload:** The digital age has made it easier to gather vast amounts of data from assessments. The challenge is in extracting meaningful insights from this data.

Reflection Questions

1. Think about a memorable assessment experience from your own educational journey. What made it memorable, and what impact did it have on your learning?

2. In your current role as an educator or instructional designer, how do you approach summative assessments and determine when to use them? Do you see any opportunities to improve their usage?

3. How do you utilize formative assessments in your instructional design process? Could they be incorporated

more frequently or effectively to enhance the iterative development of learning experiences?

4. Consider the challenges of assessment discussed in this chapter. Have you encountered these challenges in your work, and what strategies have you employed to address them effectively?

Chapter 10

The Evolving Landscape of Educational Technology

The world of education is in constant flux, driven by technological innovations that shape how we learn, teach, and design instructional experiences. In this chapter, we explore the evolving landscape of educational technology, the opportunities it presents, and the challenges it poses for instructional designers and educators.

Technology as an Enabler

Educational technology has the power to amplify learning, providing diverse tools and resources that cater to individual needs and preferences. Whether we're in a traditional classroom or an online environment, technology is the bridge that connects learners with knowledge and educators with new instructional possibilities.

Personalized Learning

> **Adaptive Learning Systems:** These systems use data and algorithms to adjust learning content in real time. They provide a personalized path for each learner based on their strengths and weaknesses.
>
> **Learning Management Systems (LMS):** LMS platforms facilitate the delivery of content and the tracking of learner progress. They enable educators to customize learning paths, provide resources, and assess performance.
>
> **Artificial Intelligence (AI):** AI is shaping the future of personalized learning. It analyzes learner behavior and performance to offer tailored recommendations, just like a personal tutor.

The Flipped Classroom

Technology has revolutionized the traditional classroom model. In a flipped classroom, learners engage with instructional content before class, often through online videos or readings. In-class time is then dedicated to active learning, discussion, and problem-solving.

> **Videos and Interactive Modules:** These can be created or curated by educators. They allow learners to review content at their own pace, ensuring understanding before class.

Online Collaboration Tools: Tools like discussion forums, video conferencing, and collaborative documents enable learners to engage with peers and educators even when not physically present.

Feedback and Assessment: Online quizzes, surveys, and formative assessments help educators understand what learners have mastered and where they need support.

Challenges and Considerations

While the possibilities are exciting, the evolving landscape of educational technology also presents challenges and considerations.

Digital Equity

Not all learners have equal access to technology or a stable internet connection. Ensuring digital equity is a fundamental challenge. It requires creative solutions and community involvement.

Privacy and Security

Protecting learner data is paramount. The digital world opens new avenues for data breaches and privacy violations. Safeguarding learners' data is a shared responsibility among educators, designers, and institutions.

Learning Distractions

> Digital tools and platforms can be a double-edged sword. While they offer resources, they can also introduce distractions. Balancing engagement with focus is a design challenge.
>
> Technology Integration
>
> Integrating technology into teaching is not a one-size-fits-all endeavor. Educators may require training and ongoing support to effectively use these tools in their teaching.

Reflection Questions

1. How has technology transformed your own learning experiences, whether in formal education or through self-directed learning? What are the most significant positive and negative impacts you've encountered?

2. Think about a time when you designed or participated in a flipped classroom or online learning experience. What elements of technology enhanced the learning journey? Were there any challenges in implementing these technologies?

3. Digital equity and privacy are critical issues in the digital age. How can educators and instructional designers work together to address these digital equity and data privacy challenges while maximizing the benefits of technology for learning?

Chapter 11

The Power of Gamification in Education

Learning, at its core, is an inherently human activity. We are curious beings, and our capacity to learn is built upon our ability to explore, experiment, and engage with our environment. So, it's not surprising that gamification, the application of game elements in non-game contexts, has found its way into education. This chapter looks into the power of gamification as an instructional strategy, exploring how it can engage learners, enhance motivation, and drive meaningful learning experiences.

The Gamification Spectrum

Gamification is a spectrum, ranging from simple game elements like points, badges, and leaderboards (PBLs) to full-fledged educational games and simulations. Here, we explore how these gamification strategies can be employed in educational settings.

Points, Badges, and Leaderboards (PBLs)

> **Points:** Points provide learners with immediate feedback and can be used to track progress. They can be awarded for completing assignments, quizzes, or other learning activities.
>
> **Badges:** Badges are visual representations of achievements. They are awarded when learners reach specific milestones, demonstrating mastery or accomplishment.
>
> **Leaderboards:** Leaderboards display learners' rankings based on points or badges. They can foster competition, encourage engagement, and promote a sense of achievement.

Educational Games

> **Immersive Learning:** Games can immerse learners in a new world, fostering experiential learning. They provide opportunities to explore, experiment, and learn by doing.
>
> **Problem-Solving:** Many educational games present challenges or problems that learners must solve. These games promote critical thinking and decision-making.
>
> **Narrative and Storytelling:** Games often feature compelling narratives. These stories can engage learners emotionally and enhance retention.

Motivation and Engagement

One of the primary benefits of gamification is its ability to motivate and engage learners. By leveraging elements like PBLs, narrative, and competition, educators can ignite learners' intrinsic motivation.

Autonomy and Mastery

Gamification provides a sense of autonomy by allowing learners to make choices and decisions. This autonomy fosters a sense of ownership over the learning process. Moreover, the pursuit of points, badges, or mastery in a game can drive learners to strive for mastery, fueling their intrinsic motivation.

Emotional Engagement

Educational games can tap into learners' emotions, making learning a more engaging and memorable experience. Whether it's the excitement of a challenge or the emotional connection to a game character, emotions can reinforce learning.

Competition and Cooperation

Leaderboards and multiplayer games introduce elements of competition and cooperation. Healthy competition can boost engagement, while cooperative play can encourage teamwork and social interaction.

Game Design and Learning Objectives

Successful gamification hinges on aligning game design with learning objectives. The game elements should enhance learning rather than distract from it.

Meaningful Rewards

Earning points and badges should feel meaningful to learners. They should not be "busywork" but should reflect progress and achievement. Learners should see the value in earning them.

Challenge and Flow

Games should strike the right balance between challenge and skill. This balance, referred to as "flow," keeps learners engaged. If a game is too easy, learners may become bored. If it's too hard, they may become frustrated.

Feedback and Assessment

Games should provide immediate feedback. This feedback helps learners understand where they went wrong and how to improve. It supports formative assessment and self-regulation.

Gamification in Practice

The successful implementation of gamification in education requires careful planning and consideration of the learners' needs, the learning objectives, and the context. Educators must strike the right balance between the game elements and the instructional content.

Reflection Questions

1. Have you ever experienced gamification in education, either as a student or as an instructor? How did it impact your motivation and learning experience?

2. Think about your favorite game or gaming experience. What elements of that game do you believe could be integrated effectively into an educational setting? How might they enhance learning?

3. Gamification has the potential to motivate learners through rewards, competition, and autonomy. What considerations should educators and instructional designers keep in mind when deciding whether to use gamification in a specific learning context?

Chapter 12

The Digital Learning Landscape

The educational landscape has been fundamentally transformed by the integration of digital technologies. From e-learning platforms and online courses to interactive multimedia resources, technology has opened new frontiers for teaching and learning. This chapter explores the digital learning landscape, examining how technology is reshaping education, expanding access to knowledge, and offering innovative ways to engage learners.

The Evolution of Digital Learning

To understand the current state of digital learning, it's essential to look back at its evolution. Digital learning has come a long way, from early experiments with computer-based training to the modern online learning ecosystem.

Early Computer-Based Training

Computer-based training (CBT) systems emerged in the 1960s and 1970s. These systems enabled learners to access content and instructions on early computer terminals.

The Advent of the Internet

The rise of the internet in the 1990s marked a significant turning point. E-learning platforms and online courses became accessible to a global audience.

Learning Management Systems (LMS)

The 2000s witnessed the proliferation of Learning Management Systems (LMS) like Moodle, Blackboard, and Canvas. These platforms facilitated the organization and delivery of online courses.

MOOCs and Open Educational Resources

Massive Open Online Courses (MOOCs) gained popularity in the 2010s. These free, open-access courses attracted millions of learners worldwide. Open Educational Resources (OER) further expanded access to educational content.

The Emergence of EdTech

The 2010s and 2020s saw the rise of Educational Technology (EdTech) startups. These companies introduced innovative solutions, from AI-driven adaptive learning to virtual reality (VR) simulations.

The Benefits of Digital Learning

Digital learning offers numerous advantages, making it an attractive option for students and educators alike.

Accessibility and Flexibility

One of the primary benefits is accessibility. Learners can access digital resources from anywhere, breaking down geographical barriers. The flexibility of online learning accommodates diverse schedules and learning paces.

Interactivity and Engagement

Digital learning often incorporates multimedia and interactive content. Videos, simulations, and gamified elements engage learners and enhance comprehension.

Data-Driven Personalization

Learning platforms can collect and analyze data to personalize learning experiences. Adaptive learning systems adjust content based on learners' progress and needs.

Lifelong Learning

Digital learning encourages lifelong learning. Learners can acquire new skills and knowledge at any stage of life, enhancing career prospects and personal growth.

Challenges and Considerations

While digital learning offers numerous advantages, it's not without challenges.

Access Disparities

Not all learners have equal access to technology and the Internet. Bridging the digital divide remains a significant challenge.

Technological Hurdles

Learners and educators must navigate various tools and platforms. Digital literacy and tech support are critical.

Maintaining Engagement

Maintaining engagement in digital environments can be challenging. Educators must employ effective strategies to foster participation.

The Role of Educators

Educators must adapt to digital teaching. This transition involves rethinking pedagogy, instructional design, and assessment methods.

The Future of Digital Learning

As technology continues to evolve, the future of digital learning holds exciting possibilities. While emerging technologies will continue to shape educational landscapes, we must remember that technology is merely a tool - human educators remain at the heart of impactful learning experiences.

Personalized Learning

Advancements in AI and data analytics will enable highly personalized learning experiences.

Virtual Reality and Augmented Reality

Immersive technologies like VR and AR will transform learning, providing realistic simulations and interactive experiences.

Lifelong Learning Ecosystems

Lifelong learning will become integral to personal and professional development, supported by a global ecosystem of digital resources.

Global Collaboration

Digital platforms will facilitate global collaboration among educators and students, transcending borders and cultures.

Ethical Considerations

As digital learning becomes more prevalent, ethical concerns related to data privacy, security, and content integrity must be addressed.

Reflection Questions

1. Reflect on your own experiences with digital learning. What advantages and disadvantages have you encountered? How has digital learning impacted your learning journey?

2. Consider the future of education. How do you envision technology and digital learning evolving over the next decade? What opportunities and challenges do you anticipate?

3. As digital learning becomes increasingly prominent, ethical considerations become paramount. How can institutions and individuals ensure that data privacy and content integrity are maintained in the digital learning landscape?

Chapter 13

The Power of Inclusivity in Education

In an ever-evolving educational landscape, the pursuit of inclusivity remains a central tenet. This chapter looks into the significance of inclusivity in education, exploring the principles that underpin it, examining its benefits, and addressing the challenges that must be overcome to foster a truly inclusive learning environment.

Understanding Inclusivity

Inclusivity in education goes beyond mere accessibility; it is about creating a learning environment where every individual, regardless of their background, abilities, or circumstances, feels welcome, respected, and empowered. Inclusivity acknowledges and accommodates diversity, recognizing that every learner is unique.

Principles of Inclusivity

Inclusivity is grounded in several key principles:

> **Respect for Diversity:** An inclusive education system values and respects the diversity of its learners. It recognizes that differences in culture, background, abilities, and perspectives enrich the learning experience.
>
> **Equal Opportunities:** Inclusivity ensures that all learners have equal opportunities to access education and succeed academically. It eliminates discrimination and disparities based on race, gender, socioeconomic status, or disability.
>
> **Universal Design for Learning (UDL):** UDL is a framework that guides inclusive education. It emphasizes providing multiple means of engagement, representation, and expression to meet the diverse needs of learners.
>
> **Collaborative Learning:** Inclusivity encourages collaboration among students, teachers, and parents. Open communication and teamwork are fundamental to supporting the success of all learners.

The Benefits of Inclusivity

Inclusivity yields a wide array of benefits that extend beyond the realm of education. These benefits positively impact learners, educators, and society as a whole.

> **Improved Learning Outcomes**

In an inclusive environment, all students are given the opportunity to succeed. Differentiated instruction tailored to individual needs can lead to improved learning outcomes.

Fostering Empathy

Interacting with peers from diverse backgrounds and abilities fosters empathy and a deeper understanding of the world. This helps learners develop vital life skills.

Breaking Down Barriers

Inclusive education breaks down societal barriers. It promotes social cohesion, reduces stigmatization, and supports the inclusion of marginalized groups.

Personal and Professional Growth

Educators who adopt inclusive teaching practices report personal and professional growth. It expands their teaching repertoire and deepens their connection with students.

Challenges and Considerations

While the benefits of inclusivity are undeniable, implementing inclusive education practices comes with its challenges.

Adequate Resources

Inclusivity often requires additional resources such as assistive technologies, specialized training, and support personnel. Ensuring these resources are available can be a challenge.

Professional Development

Teachers need to continually develop their skills to provide inclusive education. Professional development and ongoing training are essential.

Changing Attitudes

Overcoming attitudinal barriers and dispelling biases surrounding inclusivity can be a difficult but necessary task. An inclusive school culture starts with a change in mindset.

Strategies for Inclusivity

Practical strategies can be implemented to foster inclusivity in education.

Differentiated Instruction

Teachers can employ differentiated instruction methods to cater to the diverse needs and learning styles of their students.

Flexible Learning Environments

Flexible learning environments that offer various seating arrangements, resources, and tools accommodate different learning preferences.

Peer Support

Learners can benefit from peer support systems, where students support each other in their learning journeys.

Parent Involvement

Parents can play a crucial role in promoting inclusivity. Engaging with parents and involving them in school activities can create a more inclusive school community.

> ### Inclusivity Beyond the Classroom
>
> Inclusivity extends beyond the classroom into all aspects of education, including curriculum design, assessment, and school policies.
>
> ### Curriculum Design
>
> Inclusive curriculum design ensures that the content is representative of diverse voices and experiences. It provides a more comprehensive and enriching educational experience.
>
> ### Assessment Practices
>
> Inclusive assessment practices take into account varied abilities and learning styles, offering alternative methods of assessment to accommodate all students.
>
> ### School Policies
>
> Inclusive school policies should be put in place to guarantee that diversity and inclusivity are consistently upheld within the school community.

Reflection Questions

1. Reflect on your own educational experiences. How have you encountered inclusivity or the lack thereof in your schooling? How did it affect your learning journey?

2. Imagine an ideal educational environment. What characteristics and practices would define it as truly

inclusive? What benefits might it offer learners, educators, and the community?

3. Inclusivity is an ongoing journey. Consider what you can do, whether as a student, educator, or community member, to promote inclusivity in education. How can you contribute to creating a more inclusive learning environment?

Chapter 14

Building Collaborative Partnerships in Education

Collaborative partnerships between educational institutions, parents, and the community play a pivotal role in enhancing the quality of education and fostering a positive learning environment. This chapter explores the significance of collaborative relationships in education, the principles that underpin them, and the potential benefits they offer. We will also discuss practical strategies for building strong partnerships and the challenges to be overcome.

The Importance of Collaborative Partnerships

Collaborative partnerships bring together educators, parents, students, and community stakeholders to collectively contribute to the educational process. These partnerships serve as bridges connecting the classroom to the broader community. They are built on the foundation of shared responsibilities and the common goal of improving educational outcomes for all learners.

Key Principles of Collaborative Partnerships

Several key principles underpin collaborative partnerships in education:

> **Shared Responsibility:** Collaborative partnerships involve shared responsibility for students' learning and well-being. All stakeholders have a role to play in creating a supportive and enriching learning environment.
>
> **Open Communication:** Effective communication among partners is essential. It involves active listening, open dialogue, and the exchange of information, ideas, and concerns.
>
> **Mutual Respect:** Mutual respect fosters positive interactions and trust among partners. Respect for diverse perspectives and experiences is central to the success of collaborative partnerships.
>
> **Alignment of Goals:** Partners in education must align their goals and expectations to ensure that all efforts are directed towards the same vision of student success.

The Benefits of Collaborative Partnerships

Collaborative partnerships in education offer a range of benefits, enhancing the educational experience for students, educators, and the community.

Improved Student Outcomes

Research has consistently shown that collaborative partnerships positively impact student outcomes. They can lead to increased student achievement, higher graduation rates, and improved behavior and attendance.

Enhanced Parental Engagement

Collaborative partnerships provide opportunities for parents to become more actively engaged in their child's education. Engaged parents are more likely to support their child's learning and academic success.

Community Support

Collaborative partnerships foster community support for educational initiatives. Local businesses, organizations, and community members can contribute resources and expertise to support schools and students.

Professional Development

Educators benefit from collaborative partnerships by gaining access to professional development opportunities and resources. They can learn from community partners and other educators to improve their teaching practices.

Building Strong Collaborative Partnerships

Creating and maintaining collaborative partnerships in education requires intentional effort and strategies.

Identify Key Stakeholders

The first step is to identify key stakeholders, including parents, teachers, students, community members, and local organizations. Recognizing the diversity of potential partners is essential.

Establish a Shared Vision

Partners should work together to establish a shared vision for student success. This shared vision forms the basis for collaborative efforts.

Effective Communication

Open and effective communication is critical. Schools should provide multiple channels for communication and seek feedback from partners regularly.

Define Roles and Responsibilities

Each partner should have a clear understanding of their roles and responsibilities. Defining these roles helps prevent misunderstandings and conflicts.

Promote Engagement

Partnerships should promote active engagement from all stakeholders. This can include attending school meetings, participating in community events, and volunteering in schools.

Celebrate Successes

Acknowledging and celebrating successes, both small and large, helps maintain a positive partnership and reinforces the value of collaborative efforts.

Challenges and Considerations

While collaborative partnerships offer numerous benefits, they are not without challenges.

Overcoming Barriers

Overcoming potential barriers, such as differing expectations, lack of resources, or communication difficulties, is a continuous challenge in maintaining strong partnerships.

Ensuring Equity

Partnerships should be equitable, ensuring that all voices are heard and all students benefit. Mitigating systemic inequities is a vital consideration.

Cultural Sensitivity

Being culturally sensitive and understanding diverse perspectives is essential for effective collaboration, especially in a diverse community.

Reflection Questions

1. Reflect on your own educational journey. Have you experienced the benefits of collaborative partnerships between your school, parents, and the community? How did these partnerships impact your learning and development?

2. Imagine a school where collaborative partnerships are fully embraced. How would this school differ from your past experiences, or from schools that do not prioritize collaboration? What would the students' experiences be like?

3. Reflect on your own role in education, whether as a parent, student, educator, or community member. What can you do to contribute to building and maintaining strong collaborative partnerships in your educational community? How can you help address the challenges and barriers to collaboration?

Chapter 15

Evaluating Instructional Design Projects

In our journey through the world of instructional design, we've explored the intricacies of designing effective educational interventions, aligned them with the vision and mission of educational institutions, and looked into the strategies and partnerships that enhance learning experiences. As we near the end of our exploration, it's time to turn our focus toward evaluating instructional design projects. Evaluation is the crucial process through which we measure the effectiveness of our efforts, identify areas for improvement, and ensure that our work aligns with the overarching educational goals.

The Role of Evaluation

Educational evaluation is a systematic process aimed at understanding and improving the teaching and learning process. While designing instructional interventions is the creative and strategic phase, evaluation brings in the necessary analytical and reflective aspects. It is through evaluation that we determine whether our plans, strategies and implemented solutions are achieving the desired outcomes. Essentially, evaluation in instructional design serves multiple purposes:

> **Assessment of Effectiveness**: The primary goal of evaluation is to assess the effectiveness of instructional design projects. Are students learning? Are the learning objectives met? Does the intervention enhance student performance and understanding?
>
> **Feedback Mechanism**: Evaluation provides valuable feedback to designers, educators, and stakeholders. It highlights strengths and weaknesses, guiding future improvements.
>
> **Alignment with Objectives**: Evaluation helps ensure that instructional design projects remain aligned with the broader educational objectives. It ensures that the educational mission is upheld.
>
> **Accountability**: Educational institutions often need to be accountable to various stakeholders. Evaluation data can demonstrate the quality and effectiveness of their programs.

The Evaluation Process

The process of evaluating instructional design projects typically involves several key steps:

Clarifying Objectives

The evaluation process begins with a clear understanding of what needs to be evaluated. What are the objectives of the instructional design project? What are the intended outcomes?

Identifying Data Sources

Once the objectives are clear, you need to determine what data will be collected and from where. Data sources can include student performance data, surveys, assessments, observations, and interviews.

Data Collection

This step involves gathering data from the identified sources. It's important to ensure that data collection methods are valid and reliable.

Data Analysis

Once data is collected, it needs to be analyzed. This could involve statistical analysis, content analysis, or qualitative analysis, depending on the nature of the data.

Interpretation

Data analysis leads to interpretation. It's important to connect the data to the project's objectives and goals. What do the findings mean in the context of the project's success?

Feedback and Reporting

Based on the interpretation, feedback, and reports are generated. These reports are shared with various stakeholders, including educators, designers, students, and parents.

Decision-Making

The evaluation findings often lead to decision-making. Designers may decide to revise instructional materials, educators may adjust their teaching methods, and educational institutions may refine their curricula.

Types of Evaluation

There are several types of evaluation used in educational settings. They serve distinct purposes and are often conducted at different points in the instructional design process:

Formative Evaluation

Formative evaluation takes place during the development phase of an instructional design project. The primary purpose of formative evaluation is to inform and shape the ongoing project. Designers receive feedback on prototypes, materials, and strategies, which allows for iterative improvements. Formative evaluation is highly interactive and focuses on refining the project as it unfolds.

Summative Evaluation

Summative evaluation, on the other hand, takes place after the project is completed. Its primary focus is to assess the overall effectiveness of the project in achieving its goals and objectives. Summative evaluation often involves the measurement of learning outcomes, comparing outcomes to predetermined criteria or standards.

Process Evaluation

Process evaluation examines how a project is implemented. It focuses on the implementation process rather than the outcomes. Process evaluation helps determine if the project was executed as planned, whether the intended audience received the intervention, and whether any issues arose during implementation.

Impact Evaluation

Impact evaluation aims to measure the long-term effects of an instructional design project. It examines the lasting impact on students, educators, and the institution. This type of evaluation may involve tracking students' performance over time or assessing changes in teaching practices among educators.

Reflecting on Your Work

As you navigate through your own instructional design journey, consider the role of evaluation in your projects. Think about how formative and summative evaluation might shape your designs. How can process and impact evaluation help ensure that your work has a lasting, positive effect on students and the educational community?

Reflection Questions:

1. Have you ever been a part of an instructional design project that involved evaluation? What were the goals of the evaluation, and what insights or changes did it bring about?

2. In your current or future role in education, in what ways might you leverage evaluation to improve instructional design projects? What types of evaluation (formative, summative, process, impact) might be most relevant to your work?

3. How can we foster a culture of evaluation in educational institutions, making it a natural and ongoing part of the instructional design process?

Chapter 16

Continuous Improvement in Instructional Design

In our journey through the world of instructional design, we've explored the intricacies of designing effective educational interventions, aligned them with the vision and mission of educational institutions, and looked into the strategies and partnerships that enhance learning experiences. We've studied the importance of evaluation and how it plays a crucial role in ensuring that instructional design projects are effective. As we reach the end of our exploration, we're faced with an essential concept - the idea of continuous improvement.

The Essence of Continuous Improvement

Continuous improvement is a fundamental concept in education, emphasizing the ongoing process of refining and enhancing instructional design projects. It's the commitment to learning from experiences, evaluating outcomes, and implementing changes for the better. Continuous improvement doesn't mark an endpoint; it signifies a commitment to perpetual progress.

To put it simply, instructional designers don't view their work as static and unchanging. They recognize that the world of education is dynamic, and learner needs are continually evolving. Therefore, instructional design should adapt to meet those ever-changing needs. Continuous improvement serves several key purposes:

> **Adaptation to Changing Environments:** Educational landscapes are influenced by numerous factors, from technological advances to shifts in societal expectations. Continuous improvement ensures that instructional design projects remain relevant and effective.
>
> **Optimization of Resources:** As educational resources are often limited, it's crucial to maximize their use. Continuous improvement helps identify which strategies and materials yield the best results and which ones need adjustment or replacement.
>
> **Enhancement of Learning Outcomes:** Ultimately, the goal of educational interventions is to enhance learning. By continuously improving these interventions, we enhance the educational experience and contribute to better student outcomes.

The PDCA Cycle: Plan, Do, Check, Act

One method that many educational institutions and instructional designers use to drive continuous improvement is the PDCA cycle. PDCA stands for Plan, Do, Check, Act, and it's a structured, iterative approach to solving problems and making improvements. Let's break down each stage of the PDCA cycle:

Plan

In the planning phase, you define the objectives and determine what needs to change or improve. This stage often begins with a problem or an area identified for enhancement. The planning phase includes setting goals, developing strategies, and outlining the specific steps required for implementation.

Do

During the "Do" phase, you execute the plan. This is where the changes are put into action. It's important to ensure that everyone involved understands their roles and responsibilities and that the strategies are carried out as planned.

Check

In the "Check" phase, you assess the outcomes and collect data. This is where you evaluate whether the changes have had the desired effect. The data you collect is critical for measuring the success of your project and determining whether further adjustments are necessary.

Act

The "Act" phase is where you make adjustments based on your findings during the "Check" phase. This is a pivotal step because it ensures that your project continuously evolves. You might choose to refine the strategies, replace ineffective elements, or expand successful components.

Fostering a Culture of Continuous Improvement

Institutionalizing continuous improvement in educational institutions requires a specific mindset and organizational culture. It's not just about making changes; it's about making the right changes. Here are some strategies to foster a culture of continuous improvement:

Leadership Commitment: Commitment from educational leaders plays a crucial role in setting the tone for continuous improvement. When leaders emphasize the importance of learning from experiences and making data-driven decisions, it influences the entire institution.

Data-Driven Decision-Making: Collecting and analyzing data is essential for guiding improvements. Encourage a culture where educators and instructional designers are comfortable using data to make informed decisions.

Collaboration: Continuous improvement is a collective effort. Promote collaboration among educators, instructional designers, administrators, and students. A collaborative approach often leads to fresh insights and innovative solutions.

> **Professional Development:** Offer ongoing professional development opportunities to educators and instructional designers. These opportunities should focus on emerging best practices, new technologies, and pedagogical advancements.
>
> **Celebration of Success:** Celebrate the successes and innovations that emerge from continuous improvement efforts. Recognizing and rewarding individuals or teams for their contributions can inspire further progress.

The Road Ahead

As we wrap up our journey through the world of instructional design, remember that this is just the beginning. The field of education is dynamic and ever-evolving, and so should be our approach to instructional design. Continuous improvement isn't a one-time task but a way of thinking and acting that keeps education responsive and innovative.

Reflection Questions:

1. In your experience as an educator or instructional designer, can you recall an instance where continuous improvement led to significant enhancements in the learning experience? What was the change, and what impact did it have on students?

2. How can you personally embrace continuous improvement in your role, whether as an educator, instructional designer, or administrator? What steps can you

take to create a culture of ongoing progress in your educational institution?

3. Looking ahead, what do you see as the most significant challenges and opportunities in the field of instructional design?

COURTNEE R. MORRIS

Courtnee R. Morris resides in the heart of Ohio with his beloved wife of 15 years, Megan, and their cherished daughter, Siren. His journey through the realms of education has been as diverse as it has been impactful.

Starting as a compassionate preschool teacher, Courtnee's commitment to education evolved through various roles, including latchkey teacher, Health and Disabilities Coordinator, Mentor Coach, and Nurturing Father's Coordinator. His expertise extended further as a Career Technical Education Instructor specializing in Early Childhood Education, where he inspired countless students to embark on their own educational journeys.

Courtnee's passion for shaping young minds continued to flourish as he assumed the role of Adjunct Professor for the Alternative Licensure Program, guiding aspiring educators through the intricate paths of teaching. His dedication reached new heights when he became the Director of Career and Technical Education at an inner-city High School, proving that education is not just a profession but a transformative force for communities.

Venturing into the technological landscape, Courtnee seamlessly transitioned to the role of Technology Coordinator over Instructional Design and Curriculum Development, highlighting his adaptability and forward-thinking approach to education.

Beyond the classroom, Courtnee R. Morris is a published children's book author and illustrator, infusing his creative spirit into stories that captivate and inspire young readers. His words transcend the pages, resonating as a motivational speaker, and spreading positivity and encouragement to audiences far and wide.

Above all, Courtnee is a devoted Christ follower who finds solace and purpose in his faith. His love for the Savior shapes his life, values, and the way he engages with the world. As an author, educator, and speaker, Courtnee R. Morris strives to leave an indelible mark on hearts and minds, weaving together the threads of education, creativity, and faith to create a tapestry of inspiration for generations to come.

www.ingramcontent.com/pod-product-compliance
Lightning Source LLC
Chambersburg PA
CBHW070121080526
44586CB00013B/1352